With Sassafras Tea

E.E. Sorrells

With Sassafras Tea

ISBN: 978-1-7363658-4-7 (Paperback)

ISBN: 978-1-7363658-5-4 (eBook)

Library of Congress Control Number:

Written by E.E. Sorrells

Cover image by ABIOLAGFX

First Published 2023

To my mother,

the Sun of my life

and

the moment,

my muse

Table of Contents

Sprained Hearts... I

Dumbfounded 1

Lost Motivation 1

Dry Season 2

Dancing around My Words 2

Unlovable... 3

Without My Heart 3

Regrets 4

Lucky For You... 4

Someone Beautiful 5

Good Riddance 6

High on You 7

Cities of Sadness 8

Emotional Labor 8

Bills for a Broken Heart... 9

Heart Breaker... 9

Through the Stages of My Life 10

Someone Find Me 11

A Perfect Love 12

Fat's Name 12

Productivity of Language: Love...................................... 13

Aphrodite 15

Called O. 16

A Four-Leaf Clover.. 17

Any Payment Will Do 17

Sailboats 18

I Want to be a Rainbow 19

Starlight 20

Needles in a Grape Vine 21

Spring Showers 22

Lightning Loves Thunder 22

Wondering 23

Lost Love 23

At Least I Love It 23

Too Much 24

If Dreams Came True 24

Never Alone 25

Alone at the Party 26

Do I Love You? 26

Like Yellow Leaves 27

The Snake and the Corset 27

Always the Villain 28

I Cry for You 28

I Hate the Pain 28

Because You are Beautiful 29

Glue 29

Missing You 29

Writing for You 30

Taking the Stage 31

Beauty 32

Fevers of the Mind II

What is Beauty to the World 33

My Stupidity 33

Broken Filters 34

Drowning in words 34

My Captor and My Freedom 34

A Love Letter from the Voices in My Head 35

Hamsters 37

Busy 37

Memories 37

Too You 38

What They Say 38

Here They Come 39

What am I worth? 39

The Truth Will Come 40

The Villain 40

Lost and Never Found 41

Screaming 41

Hate Mail 42

It Will Get Better 42

A Love Letter to My Goldfish 43

I am Worth More 45

A Different Body 46

Clothes are for Everyone 47

A Letter to My Friend's God 48

Why are You Even Here? 50

Nausea 50

The Torture of the Past 51

Gaining Control 52

Sanity 53

What Have You Done 54

The Big What If 55

I am Still Tired 56

Is It Bad 57

Dirty Pennies 57

Instructions 58

I Would Be Lost 58

Am I Worthy? 59

Forgotten 60

I Will be There 61

I am afraid. 62

My Own Hero 63

Driving 63

Arthritis of the Soul III

I am Lost 64

Revenge 64

My Truth 64

Different Teachers 65

An Unknown Number 65

Happy for You 66

Running Away 66

Selfish Being 67

Telling You 67

Bullet Teeth 67

A Truth and A Lie 68

The Real Enemies 69

Those Who Hurt Me 72

I am a Lemon 73

Batteries 74

Papercuts 76

Therapist 76

Relics 77

Being A Victim 77

I'm tired 78

Mail in the Sunlight 79

Letters from the Nursing Home: 1 80

A Letter to My Grandmother's Southern Magnolia Tree 81

I am Surviving 82

Fear. 84

I am no Damsel 85

Too Bad 85

Stay for Me 86

Breaking 86

I Should Be 87

What the Sun Says 88

A Recurring Nightmare 89

Smiles 89

Wishing 90

i am what i am 91

What I am Worth: 2 92

Being Stupid 93

My Happiness 94

I am a Person 95

The Healing Tea IV

Look at Me 96

My Muse 96

Weapons and Shields 97

My Mini Worlds 97

Silver Dreams 97

My Hiding 98

My Perfect Body 99

0.5 Lead 101

A Love Letter to the Big Bands 102

Human 103

Mean What You Say 104

A Love Letter to Thunderstorms 105

I Deserve It 106

Tea 106

A Secret Freedom 107

Evens and Odds 107

An Arrow to Us 108

My Poetry Speaks for Me 108

A Love Letter to My Plus Sized Body 109

The Pronoun You 113

Faith of my Father 114

A Love Letter to My God 116

Brave 118

Day 367 120

A Letter to My Mother 121

The ~~Pronoun~~ Proper Noun Me 123

Flower in the Sidewalk... 124

And the Walls Came Down 125

My Body... 125

A Different Queen.. 126

My Sun 127

Parts of You 127

My Words... 128

The Sun and Moon 128

The Sunrise After Midnight... 129

Just Imagine Your Eyes.. 129

What a Start 130

Travelling... 130

Time Passes... 131

Chasing Rainbows 131

11:11.. 132

Sprained Hearts

Dumbfounded

I'm dumbfounded,

that someone with such beauty,
would cry in the mirror.

that someone with such beauty,
would spell hate on her skin.

that someone like you,
would curse their angelic body.

Lost Motivation

Where has
my motivation gone?

It has left with the will,
the will to move on.

Dry Season

Why is it,

that I can only write,

when I cry.

Otherwise

my words are dry,

emotionless letters.

Dancing around My Words

The most uncomfortable things,

I dance around in my poems:

The Pain.

The Suffering.

And what you have all done to me.

Maybe I should tell the world.

Unlovable

Why does everyone

I've ever loved,

seem to throw me away*

*maybe I am the unlovable kind

Without My Heart

What

Am

I

Without

My

Heart?

Nothing

But

An

Empty

Shell.

Regrets

I
will never
regret our
time together.

I
will always
regret not
having you.

Lucky For You

My inspiration is gone,
it left when you did.
You were my moment.
You were my muse.

Lucky for you,
I can only write so long,
before the world becomes blurry.

Someone Beautiful

How can you be so beautiful?
You take my breath from my lungs.
You dance with it like a ribbon.

But

How could you?
I know it's my fault,
for believing in love.

And

How can I move on?
Knowing I am no more
than a plaything.

Yet

I still want you.

How unfair is that?

Good Riddance

I remember,

"back in the day"

when your smile meant more to me

than the moon.

Than my own comfort.

I begged for your attention.

I begged for you.

You begged for my body.

We haven't spoken in nearly a year now.

Good riddance, I say to you.

Good riddance, my love.

Good riddance.

High on You

I'm high on you.

On your voice,

     like words of a masterpiece.

On your scent,

     like rain after a drought.

On your eyes,

     like forests I can run through.

On your smile,

     like starlight.

On your touch,

     like love but with pain embedded in it.

I'm high on you.

Cities of Sadness

When tears dry

like cement on my cheeks,

I cry harder.

Hoping that the rain will ruin

the hard work of the evil

who want to build cities

on the sadness of my face.

Emotional Labor

The giving birth

to emotions,

after a nonconsensual

love.

That painful pushing,

hoping for a newfound form,

to enter this cold

world

Bills for a Broken Heart

Paying bills for a broken heart

is expensive,

taxing,

and painful.

I cry out the payment daily.

Tear by tear

my shaky breath waivers.

But I have to pay,

Or they will just take my heart away.

Heart Breaker

I broke myself,

in a way

that should never be possible.

I broke my own heart.

Through the Stages of My Life

I think back,

to the days I cried alone.

I say that like it was in the past.

No.

It is my present.

My future holds my hopes.

My future holds my dreams.

My future holds my happiness.

Someone Find Me

I

     am

        lost

           because

        I

     want

to

     be

        found

           where

        I

     was

left

A Perfect Love

I hope you don't
have butterflies,
when she smiles at you.

They are symbols
of change.
And I hope your relationship
won't need that.

I wish you a perfect love.

Fat's Name

Why do people whisper my name?
Why do people hate me?
Why can't I be admired like *her?*
Why can't I be praised like *her?*
Why is Skinny so perfect?
Why am I so hated?

Why can't I be beautiful too?

Productivity of Language: Love

What can language not do?

It can hurt,

    it can heal,

        it can make the world change.

One word can mean many things.

            Love,

          for example

Love is love.

Whether it be between

    Friends,

        Family,

    Lovers,

        Enemies,

    Teachers,

        Preachers,

    Actions,

        Objects.

Love is love.

Though it means many different things.

Language can tell you the truth, that is how it is most productive.

Because three words mean the world: "I love you".

    Four words tear that world apart: "I *don't* love you".

Six words break my heart: "Please, don't go. I need you".

    Seven words tie me back together: "I'll be back soon, I love you".

One word means the world

                    Love.

Aphrodite

Since when was my body yours?

You act like I am a toy,

made for you,

handcrafted to please you.

      You act like the seed

      that you could put in me,

      is there to *help* me.

When I was on my knees,

I was not worshipping you.

No, I was shackled down.

My sexuality should not be defined by you.

      And it cannot be defined by you.

All you did was ruin me.

Let my inner Aphrodite thrive.

      I can please me.

            I can be me.

      I will please me.

I am my own Aphrodite.

Called O.

Take my name,

and pull it from your lips.

Don't let it hang there any longer.

My name is not a bad thing.

Stop whispering it like I am a demon,

and that saying it will summon me.

My name isn't just one thing.

My name may not be as beautiful

as your appearance.

Your heart is worse than my name could ever be.*

*my name isn't just obese

A Four-Leaf Clover

Why can't I be good enough,

for anyone but me?

I know my worth.

I know my value,

but to find someone else who does,

that is like finding a four-leaf clover,

High in the clouds.

Any Payment Will Do

When will I be paid,

for all the years of advice

I have given.

Even when I

was in my darkest place.

Sailboats

I try to make everyone happier,

than I could ever be.

I drown myself in their sorrows,

I build them a boat of my bones.

I use my skin as their sails.

Anything to see them out of the storm,

It would be worth it.

Even if I go down

without a ship

to stand on.

I Want to be a Rainbow

Why do they run from me,
everyone I have tried to love?

Is my love a storm they cannot handle?

Or a passion they would not want?

I wish they would speak,
so I could fix my raining.
And maybe be someone's rainbow.

Starlight

You were the world to me.

The stars of every galaxy,

could never outshine your smile.

The diamonds in your eyes,

were worth more than any ring.

You were made of pure gold,

to me.

You held her in the same light.

Like she was the sun.

The star that ruled your life.

Even after she burnt you a million times.

But I was nothing.

Not even the gravel

that was underneath.

Not even the grass,

you forever cut down.

I just want to be your starlight.

Needles in a Grape Vine

You told me,

that I am the problem.

That I am self-centered.

So I hid my smile.

The pictures on my phone.

I hid my emotions.

Because who would want to see that mess?

That is what your voice said in my ears.

Then I left.

But your words stayed fresh in my mind.

   Like needles on a grape vine.

    Meant to permanently harm me.

Spring Showers

It means I am growing.
That my story is not finished.

The clouds cry again.
Their gray sadness,
drifting into the pastels of sunset.

The storm isn't over,
It just no longer harbors thunder.
Now it is soft spring showers.

Lightning Loves Thunder

The clouds are angry in the summer.
I sit and watch them roll.
My tea is warm as I sip at it,
listening to the storm's cries I've learned:
Lightning loves Thunder,
but I am not sure he feels the same.

Wondering

How do I write my heart out,

when you still have it in your hands?

I will always wonder that.

Lost Love

If I scream your name to the stars,

they would never listen.

Lost love annoys them.

At Least I Love It

When I finally

love my body,

I have no one

to love it with

Too Much

One said selfish,

the other selfless.

They both said I was too much.

How do I know what to do,

when it feels like everyone is against me?

I just wish someone were on my side.

All I have is the Sun.

If Dreams Came True

i

just

want

you.

not

the

dream

i

made

Never Alone

I am not alone in this.

I can't be.

There must be thousands like me.

Hurting over a pain that

seems to last forever.

Crying over the same shattered dreams

over and over.

We never are alone,

We all look at the same midnight moon.

We all bite our tongues to keep quiet.

Because what good is it to speak out,

when only We listen?

Alone at the Party

I always watch from the sideline.

Never a part of the party.

Never a part of the game.

It's not that I haven't tried.

It's that no one wants to play with me.

No one wants to dance.

Do I Love You?

My words are pulled out,

by a string.

"I love you" I say.

As it passes through my lips

like vomit on a summer night,

I wonder If I mean it,

or just want to

Like Yellow Leaves

I fall for you,

like leaves when they yellow.

The only difference is,

they're not meant to fall this fast.

The Snake and the Corset

My breath hurts.

Each intake like a corset.

Each outtake,

a snake wrapped around my abdomen.

It is no virus.

No death wish for the future.

Just tears,

harming my way of life.

Just emotions becoming too real.

Just my future slowly slipping away.

Always the Villain

Why am I

Always the villain,

Even in my own fairytale?

I Cry for You

I cried a sea for you.

You sailed to land,

where *she* could stand.

And you both could forget me.

I Hate the Pain

At least you never

hurt me like

they loved

to

Because You are Beautiful

What would

it take,

To create that

smile of yours

Glue

If I could steal back my heart,

Glue back the broken pieces.

I would.

But I gave it to you.

So why should I want it back?

Missing You

I miss a happiness I have never felt.

I miss a love I have never found.

I miss sadness that once controlled me.

I miss a pain I never want to feel again.

I miss feeling alive.

29

Writing for You

I write about you.

You may never know,

you don't like poetry much.

I would write a world for us to live in,

if that is what you wanted.

I would write people to life,

write myself to death,

anything to keep you happy.

Taking the Stage

Time ticks by,

Like the soft song of a piano.

The rain falls,

Like a steady beat.

I cry,

Like a solo.

I smile,

As my bow.

Beauty

Beauty comes in all forms.

Whether it be printed on the skin,

Or in a book.

On the clouds,

Or in every love-struck look.

The tattoos on the clouds,

Printed there

In the memory

Of the angels.

People always seem to forget.

Fevers of the Mind

What is Beauty to the World

What is beauty,

to the blind?

It is an orchestra,

singing out sweet sorrowful notes.

What is beauty,

to the deaf?

A sunrise,

shining in the distance.

What is beauty,

to the world?

Nothing.

My Stupidity

Only I am stupid enough,

to tell you the truth.

and run you away.

Broken Filters

Why must I say everything?

My filter has broken.

Now the fish swimming inside of me die.

Drowning in words

What would I do,

without people like you,

floating around in the universe

of my life?*

*I would drown in my own words

My Captor and My Freedom

My silence,

is my captor no longer.

My words,

they are my freedom.

A Love Letter from the Voices in My Head

We know you.

Your hopes,

dreams,

wishes.

    Your nightmares,

    fears,

    troubles.

We break you down,

Selling your soul bit by bit to the highest bidder.

    sometimes to those who don't bid at all.

We like seeing you cry.

    Like waterfalls from those ocean eyes.

We tear you apart,

cutting you down,

    like the strong oak you pretend to be.

You fall,

    with a crash that shakes your own being.

We tell you the lies like truths.

We whisper in your mind,

    like a song you can't name.

We are always there,

    but you can never find us.

We are your hidden angels,

We tell you the harsh truths,

    tell you what you *need* to hear.

Tell you what pain you deserve.

    You deserve it.

   -   Your Friends, Your Enemies

Hamsters

I am like a hamster.

I run forever,

On a wheel that never goes anywhere.

Busy

They are too busy for you.

No, they just don't want you.

Or maybe,

they're replacing you.

You mean nothing to them.

Why can't they just be busy?

Memories

Memories are

but love

letters from

the mind.

Too You

No one could want you.

No one would want you.

You are too much

—Too you—

For anyone to want you.

Maybe that's a good thing.

What They Say

They don't want you.

It's all a lie.

It's all a ploy to use you.

They don't want you.

How many times have you said this,

and been wrong?

Here They Come

You have no home.

No place you belong.

No place to relax.

Stay alert.

Here they come.

I have a home.

I am where I belong.

I just need to relax.

Here they come.

What am I worth?

What are you worth?

Say it aloud:

I am worth nothing.

Worth nothing.

Worth nothing.

But I am worth everything.

The Truth Will Come

"I'm fine."

Say it again.
Slower.
The faster you say it,
the more likely they'll know
that you've been lying the whole time.

"Actually, I'm not."

The Villain

I hum a sweet tune,

Hoping maybe you will fall for me,

Like the princesses in the movies.*

*but maybe i'm the villain

Lost and Never Found

Nothing is worse

than the feeling of being lost

But

The feeling of never

being found.

Screaming

I wish

that I could scream

at the top of my lungs

for a thousand years.

Maybe then

the world would understand

what I've been living with

deep inside my head.

Hate Mail

The Hate Mail
    I get from my own mind,
is worse than anything
    anyone has ever said to me.

I write myself Love Letters in hopes
    that one day I can drown out
the harsh words that swim in my head.
    It never works for more than a week.

It Will Get Better

I am not okay.

I am not smiling.

I am not who I thought I would be.

I had such high hopes for myself.

I failed even me

A Love Letter to My Goldfish

One of you looks like a koi fish,

the other has been missing for a few days.

I am worried for him.

Fish introduced me to death.

Now I am nearly numb to it.

I have been to enough funerals,

more than people twice my age.

So why would my goldfish affect me?

I am not sure.

Maybe,

it is because that in becoming so numb,

I become so attached.

That every small thing hurts me.

But.

I love my goldfish.

They are pretty.

And their fish tank lights up my room at night.

They protect me from the monsters in the shadows.

To my goldfish,

I say,

You are beautiful.

And thank you for protecting me.

I am Worth More

You are worth less

than the clouds above you.

    At least a cloud's tears are worth something.

        At least pretty thinks can come from the clouds.

You are worth less

than the grass around you.

    At least it can be used for something.

        At least it can help others.

You are worth less

than the dirt beneath your feet.

    At least dirt has a use.

        At least nice things can use the dirt.

But I am worth more

than the voices in my head.

    At least I can be strong.

    At least I can act strong.

A Different Body

What were you supposed to be,

    if you had been graced with a different body?

How dare you say such a thing?

My body is beautiful,

    even when I feel like I am not.

My body is strong,

    even in my weakest moments.

My body is perfect,

    as perfect as it can be for me.

How dare you say such a thing?

Clothes are for Everyone

Crop tops,

      am I pretty enough to wear you?

Skinny jeans,

      do you really care if I'm skinny?

Bodycon dresses,

      am I too curvy to be seen with you?

Colorful leggings,

      do you want me to avoid you?

I don't hear a response,

because

clothes

can't

talk.

A Letter to My Friend's God

Dear god (with a lowercase "g"),

You are my friend's god.

Someone I will not worship.

Someone I will not follow

And

You are someone who fascinates me.

They say you are real.

They worship you.

But

I do not believe in you.

I have my God,

with a capital "G".

Yet

You are interesting.

I want to know more

About you and me.

And

I know you can't help me,

but I am the curious kind.

Are you real?

But

I don't want to know.

I just want to hear.

Do not show me your presence.

Because

I'll say again.

I have my God,

with a capital "G".

Why are You Even Here?

Why are you even here?

   Why is it that you're always in the way?

Why are you even alive?

   Why would anyone care,

      if you ever disappeared?

So many "why's".

So many answers that

   you don't even know.

Why are **you** even here?

Nausea

Like my mind getting sick.

The writing of its memories,

tossed out.

As though they never belonged.

The Torture of the Past

I torture myself,

    with past decisions.

I let the past pry my nails up,

    break my arms and legs,

        cut my stomach,

            twist my organs,

        pull my limbs away,

    keep me in the dark,

it knows me all too well.

I stand,

on broken bones,

and erase them from my mind.

Until next time.

    Until next time.

Gaining Control

Why do you stay here?

  This place does not want you.

    You do not belong here, not now, not ever.

  Go away, run as fast as you can.

Go away.

I will stay if I want to.

  You no longer hold a power above my head,

you no longer hold power **in** my head.

  You do not belong here.

    Go away, run as fast as you can

    Go Away.

Sanity

Sanity.

Is on the list of what I don't believe in.

Right beside leprechauns and giants.

Sanity.

Like an imaginary word,

Created by great authors of the past.

Sanity.

Like a made-up game,

Played only by adults.

Sanity.

Who wants to be sane?

Only a maniac would.

What Have You Done

Your voice.

Your screams.

Your fists against my door.

It's stuck with me.

I hear it in the thunder.

I hear it in every slammed door.

I hear it in every angered voice.

But I will always love you.

The Big What If

What if,

I could make You smile?

What if,

I could make You happy?

What if,

I was the answer to Your problems?

And what if.

You would never know me?

I am Still Tired

I am tired.

Tired of everyone.

Tired of being thrown aside.

Of being cried to.

I am tired.

Tired of being told the problems of the world.

I have my own problems.

I have my own hell.

I am tired.

Tired of not being loved.

Tired of having to write my pain out.

I am just tired.

Is It Bad

is it bad:

this anger?

this pain is breaking me.

but i stand strong.

not for me,

but for everyone who so easily,

lives without me.

Dirty Pennies

I know I am worth

the world and more.

But why do you treat me

like I am not worth more

Than some dirty penny.

Instructions

My stomach

Lives in my throat.

My spine in my stomach.

My mind on my spine.

I collapse on myself

Hoping that someone will rebuild me,

When only I have the instructions.

I Would Be Lost

I cry of the thought of you.

Just because I don't know,

how will I survive

without you.

Am I Worthy?

What have I done wrong?

Have I angered my God?

Have I hurt more people than I have tried to heal?

Have I just been seeing through blind eyes?

Someone speak out,

I beg.

Let me know my worth.

I beg.

Show me I am worthy of love.

Forgotten

What if one day,

I am forgotten?

Never mentioned by name,

by thought,

by happy memory.

What if I never

bring smiles to faces,

tears to eyes?

What if I am erased from history,

like you seemed to erase me from your mind

I Will be There

My eyes burn,

from midnight daydreams.

From thoughts I want to make

into my reality.

The things I pray for,

I play in my mind,

like a broken record.

      Like a broken record.

Staying just out of reach.

At the other end of the room.

All I must do is stand.

And I will be closer.

Step by step,

      Moment by minute,

           And I will be there

I am afraid.

What if my voice is never heard?

What if my voice is lost among the masses?

What if my voice is silenced?

What if I sew my own lips shut?

but

What if I yell?

What if I force to be heard?

What if I cry out in a way I never have?

What if I call out in the night?*

*voices afraid to be heard

My Own Hero

Why do I wait,

For a prince in shining armor?

For a rescuer,

To save me from my life?

I should be my own hero.

I should save myself for once.

Driving

I sat shotgun for so long,

I forgot one day I would have to drive.

Arthritis of the Soul

I am Lost

I feel lost
in a world that only ever
wants to feel found

Revenge

What wouldn't I do,
to ruin your life,
the way you ruined my mind.

My Truth

To think,
I almost broke
your precious heart,
just by telling you my truth.

Different Teachers

You taught me:

no means yes.

I am a toy.

I am for only your pleasure.

I taught myself:

no means no.

I am a goddess.

I am only meant to please myself.

An Unknown Number

I stayed silent,

for so long.

How many people did I let you hurt?

Happy for You

I am happy,
for you.

This is a lie,
that is permanently on repeat,
deep within my mind.

I am happy,
for you.

Running Away

I wish,
I could run away.

Run away from this world.

Away from these people.

Away from my heart.

I just want to run away.

Selfish Being

I am tired of living for you.
I want to live for me.
I want to be selfish

I want to waste my money on myself.
     Instead of buying things for others.
I want to be myself.
     Instead of being a "me" for others.

I want to be selfish.

Telling You

When I finally told you,
I write most about you.
I was afraid
You would hate me.
Seems you like the attention.

Bullet Teeth

No
was shot through my mouth,
like pearly bullets made of teeth.

But *Yes* was all you heard.

A Truth and A Lie

You looked at me.

You are beautiful, you would always say.

Lies.

Lies like moths fluttering from those
lips,
I learned to hate.

Like you.

You are beautiful, I say to myself.

Truth.

The Real Enemies

I wish that depression were a man,

and that I was were covered in bruises.

Maybe then,

people would realize:

I am badly beaten.

I am losing the fight.

I wish that the invisible injuries would show

so that people may know

the abuse I live through.

So they may see my real enemies,

because my anxiety is real,

and he is stronger than I ever seem to be.

My mind swallows me whole,

and I am trapped

in the entrails of my enemy.

I am burned by the stomach acids

and I don't know how to swim.

I am drowning.

He spits me out,

like chewed tobacco.

Like I leave a bad taste in his mouth,
but he is addicted.

My enemies look down at me,
they laugh,
they know they are stronger than me.
They know I can't stand up on my own.

Until one day,
when I did.

You should have seen
the fear in their eyes,
the disgust in my power.
They shouted at me
all those horrible words they always do.

I brush it off,
like dirt on a pretty white gown.
It hurts,
but I can still keep my pace,
stomping closer to them.

I yell back at them:
"You think you have seen power?

You think you have seen pain?"

And in that moment,
I released my inner goddess,
I freed myself from their shackles,
I am more than bumps and bruises,
I am everything they say I am not.
I am my own hero.

Those Who Hurt Me

You stare at me.
Like I am a doll in a window,
the week before Christmas.

Your hands wander across my body,
looking for the treasure
to make me sing for you.

You like my voice,
but not my mind.
just the songs I sing for you.

Am I just the candy you eat
between your meals?

Why was I never enough?

I am a Lemon

The last place I want to see you,

is my funeral.

You don't deserve to mourn me.

I am still bitter,

like a Lemon.

Sour because I am in season.

I bloomed from pain.

Blossomed from suffering.

And I am as sweet as I can try to be.

But every Lemon,

is a little sour.

I still am.

Batteries

If a child doesn't know how to write,
the world teaches them.

If a child doesn't know how to read,
the world teaches them.

If a child doesn't know how to love themself,
the world throws them away

Like they are trash,
less than paper waste that can be recycled.
No,
As though they are batteries.

Some may be repurposed,
but depending on where they are,
some are tossed into the waste bin.
Thrown away by society.

"It's all in your head"
Is never a good enough excuse.
So what?
If their brain doesn't work

the neurotypical way,

they are just a loss in the production

line?

They are punished

for something as normal to them,

as chaos to you.

They can't control it.

They can't control how society

made them feel as though

they are worth less than broken batteries.

But

if a child doesn't know how to love themself.,

the world throws them away.

Papercuts

The rain falls steadily

down my face,

It is manmade.

By boys who will never see the worth,

of the Goddess

as I stand before them.

Their words trying to cut deep.

But even paper cuts hurt.

Therapist

When will i

get paid

for being

the therapist

You never had

Relics

You surround my mind,

    like chains of thoughts.

I lock them together,

    in hopes that you will not cut me down.

Like I am an old relic,

    that was never meant to be built there.

Being A Victim

I sigh,

with the breath

of thousands of Victims,

hiding behind each word.

I'm tired

Why

  Can't

    I

      Feel

        Wanted?

It's

  A

    Never

      Ending

       Staircase.

And

  My

    Legs

      Are

       Hurting.

Mail in the Sunlight

I wait on the mail each day.
Sometimes,
the only way I feel the sunlight,
is when I walk to the mailbox.

I never expect anything special.
Usually bills to pay.
Maybe things that I do not know
if they are important or not:
things I see myself in.

And I still wait on the mail.
It never comes at a consistent time.
But that's fine.
I don't mind.
At least I see the sunlight.

Letters from the Nursing Home: 1

I walk the halls,

everything is silent.

Another angel walks home.

I walk the halls,

soft cries start to sing.

Another angel walks home.

I walk the halls,

whimpers of lost love echo.

Another angel walks home.

I walk the halls,

sobbing souls ring in my ear.

Another angel walks home.

A Letter to My Grandmother's Southern Magnolia Tree

I remember a few days around you,

when you were blooming.

Those pretty white flowers and your waxy leaves

enthralled me.

Lightning bugs would hide in your branches,

just out of reach.

I never really appreciated your beauty.

I don't get to see you as much.

But there is one like you at my church.

It is tall like you,

with white flowers growing on it.

I wish your flowers lasted longer.

they are so pure,

like a snow, in the summer.

I am Surviving

I have survived,

>   overcame all trials thrown in my way.

From *boys* who hurt me

>   to all noise in my head.

I have not thrived through it all,

>   my struggles still show on my skin,

>   >   and in my smile.

I say I am thriving now.

>   Nearly alive in the way I want to be.

But I am not thriving,

>   I am surviving,

>   >   in the only way I can.

I battle each night,

>   like an epic of heart and mind,

>   >   like a poetic story of a grand battle.

I stray away from the light

>   hiding at the end of the tunnel

>   >   in fear of a train horn screaming my name.

But I am strong,

I have healed from all my battles,

       preparing for battles yet to come.

I am surviving,

      in the way I want to.

Fear.

I wish,

You had no power

over me.

I wish,

You had no control

over my life.

I wish,

I was stronger

than you.

I wish,

you were afraid

of me.

I am no Damsel

Why must I beg for affection?

Why must I cry for love?

Is it really me?

Or is it the others?

Is it always going to be like this?

Or will one day my prince come find me?

I need to pull myself from the tower.

No one is coming for me.

Too Bad

I stay up,

waiting to hear from you.

Too bad,

you never want to answer.

Stay for Me

Why do I

let people into

my life when

no one wants

to stay?

Breaking

You broke my shell.

Then you broke the rest of me.

So why is it so hard for me to break you

I Should Be

Why do i,

give you heaven?

Why do i,

give you every piece of me?

Why do i,

give you more of me than i get?

Why do i,

act like i am nothing to the world?

I should be everything to Myself.

What the Sun Says

i am trash.

I cry at noon.

The Sun shakes her head.

If you are trash,
Then I am too.
If you are trash,
The world must not see,
What treasure you are to me.

A Recurring Nightmare

I sit alone in silence.

Because no one has time for me.

But they have time for her.

For him.

For anyone but me.

Because I mean nothing to them.

I mean nothing.

Smiles

I do not remember most of my childhood.

I am never sure as to why.

It is like my mind is trying to take,

What was the best time of my life away from me.

After years of thinking,

I can only remember,

What it felt like to smile

Wishing

I wish,

That one day,

I could come back home.

Back when things seemed simple.

When I didn't know death was permanent.

When I didn't beg the grim reaper

to take my hand and lead me away,

to a place where mothers and fathers

get along for more than a few hours.

i am what i am

why must i
degrade myself?

i am beautiful.

i am smart.

i am cunning.

i am stunning.

i am what the world needs.

i am what i need.

i just need to be reminded.

What I am Worth: 2

What is my worth to you, boy?

Do you not see the gold,

called my breasts?

Or the diamonds,

known as my eyes.

Do you not know,

the worth of my mind?

Something that I should never have

let you scavenge through.

You scratch at the rose quartz

of my brain.

The benevolence of my ruby heart,

should never have been opened to you.

I know my worth,

And so should you.

Being Stupid

I was asked once,

If you could change your past,

Would you?

No, my dear, I would not.

The Sun always taught me:

To be wise, you must have been stupid.

I have been stupid.

But I know,

Soon I will be wiser than I was the night before.

I will grow from every choice I make.

For better or worse,

Decisions are made.

Decisions must be made.

My Happiness

I will find my happiness.

Maybe here,

somewhere near,

maybe far from the place where I am now.

My biggest fear,

is the day I find it,

will be the day I am too late.

That bliss I've looked for,

it will find me,

when my last breath stops.

But I know.

That happiness is all around.

I just need to open my eyes

and breathe.

I need to smile for me,

live for me,

Be for me.

I am a Person

I am not

Some arcade game you can play,

Whenever you want.

I am not

Some open doors,

With a welcome mat between my legs.

The Healing Tea

Look at Me

Just your look alone,

is enough to send me

to the moon.

To fly me past every star,

every twinkling light

in your shining eyes.

To swim in the sky,

with you by my side

is my only wish tonight.

My Muse

The moment,

is my only

Muse

Weapons and Shields

My words
are my weapons,

And my pen,
my blade.

My Mini Worlds

My writing is all I have left.

My friends have gone.
My family is distant.
My life seems dull.

Until I write.

Then worlds flourish
under my fingertips.

The waterfall of life
flows from my mind.

Silver Dreams

I have
Silver Dreams
And Golden Thoughts
dancing in my mind.

My Hiding

i am tired of my hiding.
i have hid so long i forgot
what the beauty of the sun
looks like.

I am tired of My hiding.
I have hid so long I forgot
what the beauty of the moon
looked like.

I am tired of *My* hiding.
I have hid so long *I* forgot
What the beauty of *Myself*
looked like.

My Perfect Body

I have a perfect body.

maybe not for you,

but for me.

She protects me, inside and out.

She is perfect.

from

her wide hips to

her saggy stomach.

From

her thick thighs to

her flappy arms.

From

her chubby cheeks to

her long hair.

From

her beautiful eyes to

her fat lips.

From

her big fingers to

her crooked toes.

From

her scars to

her stretch marks.

I have a perfect body.

0.5 Lead

I write all my poems,

My letters,

My notes.

Everything,

With only 0.5 lead.

The thinness

lets my lettering

shine through.

My writing is messy,

but my writing is meaningful.

My writing is me.

A Love Letter to the Big Bands

I listen to you,

playing softly on my record player.

>It is teal.

I write to you.

Like I am an author in the 50's

>when reading was still the normal activity.

I sing to you,

along with the choirs that accompanies you,

>thought I am not much of a singer.

From your slow dances to your fast waltz,

I imagine what my life would be like,

>if I were born when you were popular.

Just dreams,

but no matter how young I feel,

>I love you.

Human

I'm tired of the cocktails.

I'm tired of toying with what would work

and what didn't.

I'm tired of being the tester.

Seeing "what this does"

"How that works."

I'm tired of being my own guinea pig.

I'm not a lab rat.

I am a human.

Mean What You Say

You say I am so beautiful.

>Like the sunrise in the spring,

>when the dew is still fresh

>and the earth smells like rain.

You say I am so beautiful.

>Like the shining moon in the winter,

>when the snow is soft and bright

>and the prints of the snow hare are there.

You say I am so beautiful.

>But do you mean it?

A Love Letter to Thunderstorms

Your thunder,

like a lion's roar,

echoes around me.

But I am in the grasslands alone.

Nowhere to hide.

Nowhere to go.

Your lightning,

like fireflies,

flashes across the sky.

Like in the summer,

I chase you,

hoping to catch you in a jar.

I fear you.

I love you.

Especially on hot summer nights.

I Deserve It

you

      owe

me

      the

world

      and

i

      deserve

it

Tea

I am afraid,

of living alone.

Because who would remind me to

drink my Tea?

A Secret Freedom

You lost control

and you were afraid,

because finally:

I could do everything.

Evens and Odds

Count down from one hundred.

Every even number,

say something good about yourself.

Every odd number,

say something bad.

Then you will learn to count by odd numbers only.*

*though i wish you even numbers

An Arrow to Us

i

    dream

        of

            only   ~~us~~*

        you

    every

night

*an arrow to us

My Poetry Speaks for Me

I am told,

that my poetry speaks louder

than the owls at night,

even when I fall silent.

A Love Letter to My Plus Sized Body

I,

have never loved,

You.

Not before now.

I was ashamed,

of the beauty that you are.

Your fat spilled over

the sides of my once favorite jeans

You've gained weight,

but why is that a bad thing?

I tried to change you,

by barely eating,

by exercising until I could hardly move.

But then that all changed.

And I hated you.

You changed so much.

Gained weight.

Gained figure.

Becoming beautiful in your own way.

Yet,

I never write about you,

because I am afraid

to acknowledge you.

Afraid to realize you are here.

But you are as perfect as you can be.

Like a young bird,

taking flight from the nest

for the very first time,

I spread my wings in confidence.

I could fly,

if only I would try.

I could have touch the clouds,

shaped like my thighs.

with planes tattooing the air.

It's taken eighteen years,

to not cry when

I look in the mirror every day.

It's taken eighteen years,

to smile at my pictures.

I've saved hundreds of them,

just to look back

To analyze my smile,

my cheeks,

my nose,

my ears,

my hair,

my shoulders,

my everything.

I will forever be insecure.

But the sea of insecurity,

that I float on daily,

will never stop me.

Because I have a strong boat.

I can stay steady,

as long as I look ahead.

My body is beautiful,

maybe not to me,

But to the people who see it.

Forget the people who type cruel words,

that they could never say to my face.

Because,

"Fat Girls" aren't pretty.
That's what I've heard.
Maybe not from spoken word,
but from the staring at the mall,
when I wear my skinny jeans.

That won't stop me.
I'll wear what I want.
Because my body is made to please me.

And,
To my plus sized body.
I will say it a million times,
Or until we both believe it,
You are beautiful.

The Pronoun You

You.

Pronoun.

Pronounced as:

<Your Name.>

Definition:

The person reading this.

Used in a sentence:

1. *You* are beautiful.
2. *You* are worth the world.
3. *You* are as perfect as perfect can get.
4. *You* are you, and that's all that matters.

Used in a Poem:

1. *You* are my words,
   a. My poems reborn
2. *You* are my breath.
   a. My life force.
3. *You* are my happiness
   a. But I can live without you.

You.

Pronoun.

Faith of my Father

Sunday, June 20, 2021: Father's Day

My father,

pastor of my church,

still goes to work.

He volunteers

to help a neighbor move.

He is still sore from helping yesterday.

He still preaches,

even though it is Father's Day,

and he should be celebrated.

He praises God,

with a strong and hardy voice.

He shouts and sings.

I could not do it,

I try though.

I still go to church.

Then there's the faith of my father,

To his Father:

the Father of all.

I am not like my father.

My faith isn't as strong.

At least not on the inside.

But this is his Father's world,

and to each listening ear,

he shares His love.

The faith of my father

is strong.

My father is strong.

He helps me,

sometimes when I don't want help,

but I know he means well.

And I love my father.

Maybe his faith too: I love my father.

A Love Letter to My God

Dear God (with a capital "G"),

I pray to You,

maybe not daily,

but when I need to.

I'm not sure if I believe in You.

Some days I am a firm believer,

others I doubt more than Thomas.

But

I wear my street shoes to church:

Never allowed to wear them in the school gym,

yet I wear them into Your home.

And

I am a bad child.

I don't believe You care.

Even when You show me You do.

I never know whether to praise You,

116

Or curse You for my demons.

Even though I know you didn't send them to me.

I need proof of Your existence.

I need You to show me You're here.

Whether it be in the clouds or the sun itself.

I don't know what to do.

Do I pray to You for help,

or do I fight by myself?

Give me a sign.

Show me in the most obvious way.

Take my troubles away.

Let me love You purely.

Let me love You truly.

Let me face my demons *with* You.

- a sinner

Brave

For the woman,

who walks alone at night.

You keep your keys in your hand.

Pretending to talk on the phone.

You are brave.

For the woman,

who wears a skirt on the train.

You keep pulling on it some,

in hopes that the men will stop staring.

You are brave.

For the woman,

who goes to the bar alone.

You hold your drink to your chest.

People stare at you like a butterfly in winter.

You are brave.

For the woman,

who speaks out for herself.

Your words are like fire coming from your throat.

I hope that you win all your battles.

You are brave.

For the women,

everyone that I know.

You are like flowers in the sidewalks

You can fight to win.

You are brave.

Day 367

Day 367: make up

My make up is much more dramatic now.

I no longer fear the vibrant eye palettes.

I no longer dull my blush.

Let me be my dramatic self.

Your judgement only fuels me.

A Letter to My Mother

My Mother,

So much is to be said about you.

You are the sun
to my moon.
The light that helps me shine.

You are my freedom,
My soul set free.
Your house is my safe place.

I know I can trust you.
I tell you everything.
Until I start to drown in my thoughts.

I tell myself I need to be strong,
That I must fight alone.
But then you are there, when words fill my lungs.

You are the boat,
That holds me on stormy seas.
You keep me safe.

We have jokes,

that only we understand.

I love those.

We've shared tears,

that only we know about.

They hurt.

I don't write about you much.

Only because,

I'm afraid one day these memories will be all that I have.

Mama I love you.

- your youngest

The ~~Pronoun~~ Proper Noun Me

Me.

~~Pronoun.~~ *Proper Noun.*

Pronounced as:

> *E.*

Definition:

> *The person writing this.*

Used in a sentence:

1. I am *me* in the best sense possible.
2. I am the *me* I want to be.
3. I am the *me* I strive to be.

Used in a poem:

1. I am the *me* of my dreams,
   a. the *me* I have always strived to be.
2. I am the *me* I need,
   a. the *me* I deserve to be.

Me.

~~Pronoun.~~ *Proper Noun.*

Flower in the Sidewalk

You will never see me,

as the person I am.

That hurts more than a knife.

Why can't you see me,

for who I am now?

Not as who I once was.

I have grown,

like a flower out of concrete.

I am strong.

I am beautiful.

I am unique.

And I will not be stepped on any longer.

And the Walls Came Down

Break my walls down.

I bought a hammer for you.

It may take time to break through.

But I will treat you as a hero.

Because you will be.

My Body

My stretch marks,
are but love marks,
left by the angels.

My scars,
are battle wounds,
proving that I can survive hell,
and make it to heaven.

A Different Queen

You claim,
I am different.

You claim,
I am not good enough.

You claim,
No one will ever want me,

I say,
"Darling, you are perfect.
The sun herself is jealous.
The moon would bow to you.
If you are what difference is,
Then normal is horrific.
You are my goddess.
My queen.
My reason to keep smiling."

My Sun

I cannot write about you.

Not because you've hurt me

Simply because I love you that much.*

*to my mother, sun of my life

Parts of You

Thunder rolls in the distance,

Lightning cries for his love.

Rain kisses the tree leaves,

Wind tickles the crops.

The world is in love.

I hope you are too,

Not with someone else.

But the parts of you.

My Words

I don't want to last forever.

But I want my writing to.

I want my words to float in the sea,
to last much longer than me.

How absurd,
to think my words would last for years
past my death,
and prove my worth once I'm gone.

That would mean the world to me.
Just to see,
That I have been successful.

The Sun and Moon

I love the Sun.
Because what is the moon
Without her?

The Sunrise After Midnight

Pain has ruled my life for years.

I have relied on it to feel alive.

I want to let go of the ropes,

I held on too long.

The rope burns are numb,

the scars are healing,

like little stories on my skin.

I do not need you,

I need me.

I need myself to see past the pain,

To see past the bad,

And to see the sunrise after a silent midnight.

Just Imagine Your Eyes

How beautiful is the sky,

When you look

at the same moon I am?

What a Start

Hi

The conversation started.

I remember the first time I saw you.

You were beautiful.

I was in awe.

Hi

The conversation starts.

I see you and smile.

You are beautiful.

I am in awe.

Travelling

The world

Is in your eyes.

I want to travel the world sometime.*

*come with me

Time Passes

I live by the hour.

I live by the minute.

I live by the second.

But I will live any day with you.

Chasing Rainbows

I try to distract myself,

From this looming doom.

This constant fear and pain.

But maybe I am in the eye of my biggest storm.

Maybe my promised rainbow is just a few minutes ahead.

11:11

Make a wish,

make it count.

Hold your breath,

and let it out.

I don't know,

what you wished.

But I know,

you are heaven sent.

CPSIA information can be obtained
at www.ICGtesting.com
Printed in the USA
BVHW012101030423
661674BV00016B/214